AFTER FAME

by the same author

poetry
81 AUSTERITIES
KIM KARDASHIAN'S MARRIAGE

prose
SAFE MODE

SAM RIVIERE

After Fame

The Epigrams of Martial

FABER & FABER

First published in 2020
by Faber & Faber Ltd
Bloomsbury House
74–77 Great Russell Street
London WC1B 3DA

Typeset by Hamish Ironside
Printed in England by TJ International Ltd, Padstow, Cornwall

A CIP record for this book is available from the British Library

ISBN 978–0–571–35692–8

10 9 8 7 6 5 4 3 2 1

Contents

Acknowledgements

Some of these poems were published in *Blackbox Manifold*, *Cambridge Literary Review*, *MAL*, *Mote*, *Murmur*, *POETRY*, *Poetry London* and *Poetry Review*. A version of [71] was published as 'Sleep' by Rhubaba Gallery, Edinburgh in 2017. Parts of 'Law and Rhetoric' appeared in *Alt-Age: Designing Belief* (Royal College of Art, 2018). Parts of 'After Fame' were first published as a pamphlet, *Preferences* (If a Leaf Falls Press, 2016). 'Further reading' makes use of a transcript of a recording of a reading given at the Other Room, Manchester, on 23 June 2016, and was published in *The Other Room Anthology 9* in 2017. Several of these poems were broadcast on *The Echo Chamber* on BBC Radio 4 in 2015. Some were published under the title 'After Martial' in *Cassette 86* (Dostoyevsky Wannabe, 2015).

A Hawthornden Fellowship in 2017 and a grant from the Society of Authors' Authors' Foundation in early 2018 assisted the completion of this manuscript.

Thanks to Daisy Lafarge, Oli Hazzard, Matt Welton, Lavinia Singer and Matthew Hollis for their attention to the poems, and to Aidan Wall for his notes on [117]. Special thanks to Mat, Sophie, Stacey, Crispin, MG, and AK, who in different ways and usually without their knowing it helped to write this book. Without my knowing it, one poem was written for C.

saepe soloecismum mentula nostra facit
MARCUS VALERIUS MARTIALIS

'*my pen is often erring . . .*'

A SLAVE READER

Eighteen of the 118 poems in this book begin with the pronoun 'I', which when printed looks identical to 'I', the Roman numeral. Welcome to *Book I* by the Roman epigrammatist Martial, which is actually at least his third book. Review copies differ subtly. These poems were designed to ingratiate their author within a particular system of expectation and reward, and the resemblance is precisely not coincidental, in that their publication here does not exceed the reaches of an economy that for once has no legal mode of revenge to exact upon its slavish copyist. This volume aims to discover whether you can game a poem's legislation from within, using opportunities both living and dead (the first person), and its inaccuracies only aid in decreasing the potential recognition of sources, accessed since 2013. There's no protection, thank god. You head out of the door and turn left, past the Greek barbers, right then right again. Poetry's at the back next to the main till. During the preface, each poem is being painstakingly replaced by its description, while the original stays in my imagination (in Latin). Then it's replaced by the description of its description, at which point we're in the reality movie business. There are no keys left, just the pitiful hope of evading obsolescence through sheer breadth of application. Specifically: no specifics. There are certain conventions you'll be aware of by now, faces that resemble fingerprints, watery light, a breathable atmosphere, and a way of proceeding through the R-shaped trees, visible from the window – there's an actual sunset happening out there, like an embarrassing thought. The names of authors are not really on the increase, rather they've been multiplied inside their ancient predecessors, abusing them so badly that they hid away all the great things they could have given us.

Then, at last, through something less valuable, weirdly, the fame of their feeling is proved to us, perhaps even 'in' us. It reveals its chest-high slogan. Far from the simplicity of bad jokes, gift tags, margin notes, erotica, desperate voicemails, discount codes, reported comments, texts from your dealer, 'your card has been declined', cocktail hacks, non-disclosure agreements, extended walkthroughs, speedy diagnoses, hot-tub assembly guides, season recaps, ancient emojis, recycled blurbs, pop quizzes, encrypted lyrics, true explanations of what you really meant, make-up tutorials, song requests, thought experiments, duplicate petitions, out-of-date wishlists, and all manner of indecipherable symbols, my translator writes improperly from a foreign book that has a clever person inside it – the covers should be treated like enormous inverted commas. Any words of truth can be left playing quietly where you found them: the language of description is useless if it appears on the object it's describing. But I should have given an example. The other titles of this book are *Summer Day*, *Nomentum*, *Intellectual Property*, *Memoirs of My Benefactor*, *No Touching*, *My Italics*, *As Material*, *Fair Use* and *Friends*. To be with me is to be anyone who's feeling exceedingly sorrowful, but even so, who better to bump into, out here among the numbered trees. I've already complained that this was done without matching any documents in Latin – I told him not to do it, in fact, but he went ahead, and I reach you, if I reach you at all, through the grave-like forms they left. Still, I can try to be content with the feelings they spell out from this angle. Epitaphs are written for those who like leftovers and to look at flowers, and I'm not listed in the programme, or in what happens after it. You've been listening to the decaying present with me, Marcus, like a friend who shares my name. When I felt the flowers stirring, I read articles on bankruptcy. And when the festive mobs and franchises visited this phoney ruin, I retreated to my coterie, to invent my other friends (a better word than 'clients'). The roof caved in on my antagonists, as they mishandled an invoice. Clouds changed a word at time. It's the permanent crisis of what to do next, I tell my scribe, who is providing his services without pay. I sign whatever he hands me.

Was that a wave?

YOUTH AND EDUCATION

[1]

Students you have offered him feelings
that few show to the ashes of a poet
with books sent around the world
and coruscating commentaries
stop looking   if you like
I almost retired   but
guess who's back
this is the law

[2]

I want to be with you wherever
paperbacks are partying
forget about your regular shows
and stop checking your phone for a second
you need a new distraction
or maybe a guide
why don't you buy a real book
and wander the city
i'm pocketsized

[3]

You like the shelf life
a solitary guy not ignored by women exactly
nor snubbed by the old marx crowd
or even snorted at at readings much
but if someone calls you a genius you get to kiss them
and ascend the rankings like an owl (*****)
now that you have glided onto fairer markets (international)
now that you have reproduced (2nd printing)
but not so often I needn't suffer erasures
contractual artistic or otherwise
I suppose you've earned that sad shaft of sky
where you flutter like an invoice
i'll go home
perhaps you're right

[4]

Drop *The Book of Eyebrows*
(I'm referring to your look)
when you choose to pick up my book.
The Book of Triumphs is a joke book.
I think I noticed your expression change
on the cover of *The Book of Laminations*.
There's no shame in lamentation,
or at least there shouldn't be, in my book.
The Book of Censorship is quite amusing
reading. *The Book of Derision* in Latin
isn't. I hope you read my book of poems
while lying supine on a crimson sofa,
with the pages resting on your eyelids,

wearing an expression like the cover (it's blank).
My life proves it – my poems are harmless.

[5]

I give you jacuzzis and lengths of luxury
you give me paper the poetry of poverty
so what we want's an inflatable book?

[6]

A rabbit hides in the wheel-arch on a flight to hawaii
and arrives alive a poem stops a tank long enough
for a picture to be taken I myself have become more
fearful of heights the question is then what happens
the eye of jupiter is growing smaller but also colder

[7]

The movie is better than the book
which is better than the experience
silver is better than gold (it doesn't infect piercings)
a fake masterpiece is better than a real one because at least
it's affordable
permadeath in virtual warfare is better than actual death in
actual warfare
imitation is better because it's sincere
whereas innovation seeks to impress

and anyway is never what it says it is
the second time is better than the first, as you well know
the remake is self-conscious and therefore more morally alert
this sentiment is better than the other times it has been expressed
because in the past it was expressed more forcefully and now it can relax
even thinking that Salinger meant David Copperfield the 1990s magician
who made real cars and buildings disappear then reappear
is better than knowing he meant Dickens
but only because others have thought this before you
and written about their mistake with winning modesty
or honesty or both
a cat hunting a bird is better now
because of cartoons
just as the cat that lives next door
is a better cat because it is not your cat any more
a rhyme is better the more times it has been used
cliché is better than truth
truth is just something that hasn't become a cliché yet
but inevitably will
(then you can put it in your pocket
and no one can put the truth in their pocket)
and any king or queen or president or prime minister
is better than all previous kings or queens or presidents or prime ministers
any poem is better than all the poems that precede it
that say essentially the same thing
which means new is better than old
but only if it looks or sounds or otherwise seems somehow old
being in a simulation is better than being in reality
watching the simulated stars set to ambient music created by a gifted recording artist

is better than watching real stars set to dismal sounds from
 real life
derivative beauty is better than any other kind
(here we are surrounded by all this derivative beauty –
 imagine!)
however the audience will still say, 'nah'
however many times you say
the cover version is better than the original
but the cover version is always better than the original
I know that the cover version is always better than the
 original
and the reason I know the cover version is always better than
 the original
is that I've never heard the original

[8]

There are strategies to keep you safe
which should be followed to the letter
just try and be sensible I guess
remain vigilant between streetlights
don't sprint down any dark corridors
or draw too much attention to yourself
be famous for starting fights and running away
or better yet deny everything you've done
I believe the police are here to protect us

[9]

A person is attractive
in the midst of things
trying to be attractive
makes you immediately
not
a guy
can only be hot
without thinking

[10]

I can offer your hand
no prayers or presents
I know it isn't fair
instead of a kiss
nothing is uglier
than getting a cough

[11]

However far in debt
you are there's always
more if I flash the card
that's stuck to my palm
or if I whisper 'money'
it comes out of the wall
I eyeball the bill even
when it isn't unpaid

capital in the abstract
I get it for my friends
as well and in the event
of the unthinkable I come
prepared with the face
and *that's impossible*

[12]

The provocations gather in gallery shadows
images of skyscrapers capped with permafrost
and steaming rivers risen round their ankles
the streetsigns snarled in ivy and honeysuckle
and here the gallery itself is depicted in ruins
run by wolves its fine shadows shot through
this show doesn't have anything left to prove

[13]

When we're together
it's a suicide pact
that may as well be
deferred indefinitely

[14]

Only in the kingdoms of Rome
or Heaven can the diabetic lion return
to the arena amid enormous cheers
now in possession of a sweet tooth
to be poisoned by a willing Christian
who gorged himself on fine wine
which reverts to sugar in his blood
clap your hands for Caesar's camera/god

[15]

Neglecting to count the hours
won't hasten or delay
the sight of white mountains
doubled in wide lakes
as the paramount logo somehow
outlasts its fading
the endurance of a theme
is a kind of afterlife
here with us today

[16]

The freedom to write bad poems
mediocre poems some good ones too
that's what a book *is* you guys
not your grandfather's freedom

[17]

They urged me to address
the issues of the day
they told me I 'nailed' it
'nailing' it is what
the coffin maker does
I think I screwed it up

[18]

Why mix the high style with the low style
what good has the high style done you
vs. what bad has the low style done
corrupt the high style I don't care
those readers need to be corrupted
but the low style is beneath derivation
it corrupts like money incorruptibly itself

[19]

Your first success lost you your friends
the second destroyed your reputation
and the third drove away your family
any further ambitions may be pursued
in total security: there's nothing else
the soliciting of happiness can cost you

[20]

Fame is such a sweet draught
dizzily it crashes the blood
or you can smoke it

[21]

The right hand pointed out a shooting star
but it was quickly re-identified as a satellite
and it was very embarrassing but unknown
to anyone and light years past that point
thanks to a major misconception the hand
had picked the planet that my reader's from
the trick might be not caring if you're wrong

[22]

Contrary to what the poets claim
when the surveillance state connects
its interlocking cells and the screens
finally resolve us the first ones to vanish
are always JOURNALISTS meanwhile
the press can hardly be bothered with books
at all let alone the armed/secret services
I suppose each will go after their own

[23]

A single look accounts for you
sent ray-like through the steam
the specific shame of nakedness
feels just like being seen through
& at the same time misunderstood

[24]

That guy was born with sharp little teeth
perhaps that's why his hair's so long
a wreck   with famous eyebrows
but relax his looks are strong
not lethal   you'd hurt him
if you were   a woman

[25]

Eat at the people with books
this is at the heart of the service of learning
there's no need to be shy in front of the elderly
at all these literary parties
where a kind of fame surely waits outside
with a little glass vial
to carry off the prize of your beauty
thereby saving you the trouble
condemned to London
you've lived so long by yourself
now start living in paper

as a flame does
(ashes are for later)

[26]

As if high on herbs of provence
this produce is commercial vintage
manufactured somewhere else
and nowhere near the shortlist
the label reads please destroy
these hideous jeans now please
it's better to own one pair than fifteen

[27]

We may have made arrangements
it was late and wasn't there wine
I once waited at an intersection
for britney or brittany for ages
it feels like the whole universe hates you
but how can you not have learned
that there are plans made when drunk
it's unseemly to remember let alone speak of

[28]

Yesterday is not yet in its box
but somehow the light
has come uncorked
would you understand
if I said the night had failed me

PUBLIC LIFE

[29]

My reputation is a book
and if you want to be my stand-in
just like I am fine
you can recite my poems
while lying on the kitchen floor at night
or you could photograph these pages
in a bookshop on your lunchbreak
but if you want to take the credit
for this style yourself
i.e. if you want to 'own' it
I'm afraid you'll have to 'buy' them

[30]

doctor killer confidant
let us lay to rest
all the selves you don't want

[31]

I promise when you cut your hair
and the curls fall
to mingle with the filthy leaves
the stares of boys and girls will arrive

like knives at your white neck
newly revealed
as if routed to their source
and with each long look
they'll style your lines again
becoming angular
as again the curls fall
your last weeks as a teenager
but slower this time
slowly like your early twenties

[32]

I don't like you
don't ask me why
I can't say anything
but 'I don't like you'

[33]

No matter what the loss is
crying while with friends
is always a performance
it's like bribing a witness
in the absence of evidence
it only counts as crying
if you're crying alone
and preferably in silence

[34]

I know for you the pleasure's
in being open and unguarded
about the things you've done
and while leaving your tracks
you imagined someone (me)
coming back to 'crack the case'
how to explain that some prefer
the truth to creep as if it were
a latticework upon a monument
(which remains implacable)
and as it is the things you say
are too likely to stir me
and too plain to imagine

[35]

I write verses for my equals
not a teacher to dictate in class
these poems' wives can't be without
a penis please or would you rather
have me write down words that say no song
who dresses in petticoats these days
anyway this law was given to the poems
of Martialis who cares unless they're
somewhat prurient you could spare yourself
the severity born of a castration complex
by letting the work stand up for itself
also don't spit my own stuff back at me

[36]

My life
is a thread
shared
by two brothers
I want both of them
to die first
(but on whose side [*submissa voce*
will my story
be stitched?)
if one fails
or disappears
the other's design
appears inevitable
is there any way
to reverse the material
to read the workings underneath
so that I was first to disrobe
before entering the river
full of active shadows
and you did your time
inside the prison
of that pattern

[37]

Art is satisfied with gold
art is satisfied with shit
that's what I call a relationship

[38]

If you sign the petition
then I'll remove my name
(the only reason you added your signature)
and if you remove yours
I suppose I'll add mine again
and it will go on like this
for a really long time

[39]

There are few here who can be counted friends
few who understand loyalty or aspire to art
few who defend and admire the virtuous
few it's simple to love and for whom
you'd happily sue and especially
few as smart as they appear
to appear and yet few
without cunning
few   if any

[40]

To the man on the train
sitting across from us
who hates to read
pleasure in her countenance
and yet strains to see
my title's stern typography

go ahead and envy us
with your livid face
in your tired new novel
like someone reassessing
their relationship having witnessed
for the first time true romance
because she hasn't even seen you
and now we've finished reading

[41]

You're not the capital's purveyor of inclement art
traversing the pale river with a glass of equally pale sulphur
on a trip in search of black ice cream
or whatever it is the russians are buying
nor an idle dealer who sports a crown of vegetables
in your self-deprecating portrait
(a little fancy commissioned
not to be indiscreet but
in the fantasy
at 'some' expense)
not even the owner in your wildest dreams of a kept viper
but more a kind of overlarge boy who somehow drags out
  a salary
on the halved lunches of interns
hoarse from smoking
not thy powerful talk
you stay in the shop to keep in the shade that's all
you are not the best urban poet
but this gallery has a heartless master on six figures
who loves to say he's all mouth and isn't
and even asks after your finances

the bastard
and why look up from your phone
at your desk at reception
when it seems
you're the only one the satire on the walls this month has
seen
(it can't cut both ways, can it?)
and nobody has ever penetrated the depths of the Mercedes
that waits
like a black moon
or a scoop of something poisoned
melting on the curb outside
ignored by wardens as if they can't perceive the gleaming
anomaly
so great is it
and you with your 'I always had a good nose for it'
you with your aquiline sophistication and games of insolence
their verve dulling let's be fair in these conditions
and your brochures
your spelling
just enough bait

[42]

Even when she's gone to bed
I still rehearse her arguments
lecturing anyone who'll listen
until their eyes have had enough
and behind me at the hotel bar
I leave the forms of her corrections
reduced to empty quotemarks
the debris of administrating drunks

[43]

Thirty over-thirties were invited to a party
  so tedious that no one would ever speak of it
helping the scene to establish its true professionalism
  as intrigues failed to ripen on the barren networks
everyone drank and many regarded their options
  I myself inspected for an hour a softening apple
watched a postgrad pair off with a flexible broom
  and when a stray pomegranate seed was discovered
it became the night's major point of discussion
  how its transience mocked the little imitation tulips . . .
Later someone showed around a fogged image of a girl
  a colleague announced she could murder an olive
I recalled a recent dream[1] and everyone listened
  because a need to see the night through had arisen
not in case someone put on that film about dwarves
  but as a task in which career prospects were levered
so at twenty to four we were still wearing our spectacles
  as the ambassador remarked to a visiting presence
with the ample disinterest we all routinely employed
  in this line of work there must be time for time off . . .

1 By the time the inn came into view it was almost dark. I was weary from the day's long ride, eager to find sustenance and shelter, and it was a relief to see its little windows lit. On the threshold, stamping my boots and steaming in the peat-scented gloom, I could see I was fortunate to have kept my appointment. Bowed over a small table, a figure was toying with a large orange tulip, a travelling cloak not entirely disguising the signs of bondage. Erotion – for it was she – quickly showed me how the papers I was carrying could be hidden inside the tulip's artificial petals to ensure safe transport. Then, sipping slowly on a mud-coloured stout, she told me

[44]

These lines are lascivious and stuffed
but also regal and scrupulous of course
only the largest and youngest bear paper
let's do   the same thing twice   but
too much Stella   it seems for you   this is
you have twice   the charm   I said the same
thing twice   too much   I did it again   oops

[45]

A book no one reads
    or unlimited sequels
  'this is just to say'
'I repeat my themes'

---

how she'd come into possession of the item. The tale[2] carried us deep into the night, and by the time I retired to my haybed in the attic I was so fatigued I felt sure that sleep would swallow me immediately. But instead I lay awake, until the sounds of the village began to fill the country air outside – observing the false flower as it rested in my hand – only its weight giving a clue as to its secret cargo.

2 Formerly the slave of a benevolent though taciturn landowner, Erotion's freedom had been promised to her in his will. On his death, however, this information was suppressed by the sickly eldest son, who had long wanted Erotion for his concubine. When the landowner's young daughter took pity and revealed his secret, Erotion plotted to escape, using the flower to conceal a copy of the will (a delicate contraption of indeterminate origin, she'd discovered it among her master's possessions following his demise), delivering it to the nearest authority and thereby winning her freedom. But after only days on the road, news of the daughter's untimely death (by plummeting from her bedchamber window) had reached her.[3] When we met, she was intent on returning to her late master's estates to exact revenge upon his wastrel son, her persecutor.

3 The messenger, a scribe, claimed to have overheard this detail at a university drinks party – by this point my colleagues had lost interest.

[46]

Unadorned with figs
you said what's the point
if you can't see anything
not the make of your shirt
you wouldn't take off
while making a face in the dark
you saw my lewd feet instead
and even 'besotted'
it was hard to continue
as if hearing *The Archers* theme
with a soft dick
on your midriff
adorned with figs
in the morning
your crepe-y ass was so interesting
slow down
or I'm done

[47]

This is to acknowledge

that poets do admin

in 2018: *received*

[48]

Saved from a certain fate
not by the master
but a nimble gift
you tossed from palm to palm
the heroine making a surprise exit
to elude her nemesis
you wouldn't win
or anything so obvious
but running rings in the sand
is not only safer
it's great for your image
if it's not done in good faith
then shut up
'and if I manage to avoid the dogs
and find refuge?'
– rabbit
it would be outlandish

[49]

It was said you would find a high level
the cars and clothes as cold and hueless as each other
the premiere slopes
on half-eaten mountains
and the secluded island
with a beach you love
its grasping shoal-waters
and the watchful stillness of the inland lakes
whose opaqueness helps you to forget the other shore
its harsh metallic aspect

green like iron or ice
but from here you can nominate the games
your mind as cloudless in the shade
as the frosted water jug
and when November comes
bringing with it your birthday
and feelings of powerlessness
this climate is yours to return to
enmeshed in the global cyclone whirl
strangely untouched
a safety born from slyness maybe
and where your legacy is laddered
but on some evening in the future
in a small wooded area beyond the ring of firelight
you will call to the stranger
who waits among the trees
with a smell recalling blueberry muffins
sudden hunger proclaiming his company
a crescent of skin revealed
by the slit in your ballgown
and the party on the beach will seem distant
its noise growing querulous like that of your many clients
having a disagreement of some sort about the government
– it seems an accusation has been made
and your presence is demanded on the carpet
if it isn't a dream
you've been sleeping all morning
in a deep pale sleep
because you are insane and deserve another philosophy
because you have success
yet do not enjoy your joy
and instead you envy every stranger
their stillness and opaqueness
and you ask them to turn out their pockets

for what remains
when the business of fame
finds a final sufficiency
and the waters fall silent

WORK AND LEISURE

[50]

If more is less
I'll finish what's left

[51]

Is it cruel to describe
the zeroing grip
thumbnail and fingernail
the knuckle and the neck
οκ? ορ μαγβε α βητ αμβητηους?

rabbit don't tempt me
who even wants it &
what bearing does that have
ψειι, γδυ'νε ζοτ μγ αττεπτηοπ

now can you or not
on your white throat show
with a vanishing breath
a worth slenderer than this
τηπγ δεατη, γου'ρε ητ

[52]

I address a rich friend, Q., and ask him, if he sees anyone circulating my poems as if they were their own, to intervene and declare their true authorship. I use the device of referring to my poems as if they were inferior interns, whom I have 'let go', but were then seduced into providing free labour for another creative professional. The idea of the poem as cast off employee, a scrounger or layabout who is easily attracted by the promises of others clearly has precedents, and I point out that the similarity between publication and dismissal from employment rests on the existence of copyright – a poet should be able to control the subsequent appearances and allegiances of their poems, just as an employer in a buyers' labour market has the power to refer or recall their workers according to demand. Poetry is supposedly strictly controlled after publication, but the advent of a network where content is often separated from its origins has allowed poems to add their value to the endeavours of another's project, i.e. to *work for them for nothing*. Q. is of course the first alphabetical character on a conventional computer keyboard.

1. The detail of Q.'s affluence (why else should it be noted?) suggests that while apparently requesting his assistance, I am actually accusing him of co-opting my works in illegal or unethical circumstances of which I am obviously aware (why else should the matter concern me?).
2–3. Feigningly, I offer Q. access to the material in question, so that he may more easily identify its misuse, as if he isn't already well-acquainted with it, etc.
3. The possibility is raised that Q. is the same appropriator of worthy causes who is attacked in 29, 38, 53 and 72 (the comparison is certainly striking). In this case 'Q.' marks an exception, as the general rule is that characters are not supposed to be identifiable. This perhaps serves to heighten the seriousness of the allegation, if we take it as such. Q. is described elsewhere as 'exemplary'.
5. (Q.'s capacity as benefactor and claimant, his identity: see *famous eyebrows*). The poem is compared variously to a pet (who 'settles in your lap'); a private chef or perhaps food taster ('poisonous inscriptions'); a visiting

critic or secret shopper who is on the premises to assess the standards of Q.'s hospitality, and who sarcastically praises the 'satisfactory service' before reporting back to the poet (somewhat confusingly) via the poem itself; and lastly a spy or double-agent, 'photographed next to an impenetrable drink'. In short, the poem reveals Q.'s invitation to act as its new agent, and turns to the poet to await a counter-offer.

8–9. In order to unfreeze the problem of the poem's loyalties, it is suggested that it is placed (imaginatively) between Q. and the poet, who both call to it, as one would in a sort-of game with one's sibling with a puppy or kitten, in order to solve a sort-of playful dispute of ownership. Q. hails the poem 'poem', or remains silent, admitting his failure to credit the work; the poet hails it 'plagiarism', or remains silent, indicating the redundancy of his appeal, and that the claim is essentially liquid. They repeat this contest three times, each time arriving at a different outcome (it never occurs that neither of them positively identifies the poem). A bystander touches them both with a wand as a provisional measure, as the poem is not actually present. From the poet's perspective, the ritual is conducted successfully if Q. agrees to renounce his curatorial role and resume that of customer or patron. The poem takes its place in a line-up of other poems of roughly equal height and character, behind one-way glass, and, opening its mouth to speak, ends abruptly – unable to deny either the appeal or the accusation.

9. The word 'plagiarism', actively avoided until the conclusion, where its contemporary usage is invented, is from *plagium*: the stealing of someone else's slave, or the forcing of a free man into slavery. In a so-called slaveless society, the irrelevance of the original word would make it easier for it to take on a new sense. Erotion was my favourite one. The poem's silence cannot appear in person.

[53]

I did two wrong and stupid things. The first concerns some people I interviewed over the years. When I recorded and typed up these conversations, I discovered something odd: things that sounded perfectly clear when you heard them being spoken aloud often didn't translate to the page. When this happened, if the interviewee had made a similar point previously in their writing (or, much more rarely, when they were speaking to somebody else), I would use those words instead. I justified this to myself by saying I was giving the clearest possible representation of what the interviewee thought, in their most considered expression.

But I was wrong. An interview isn't an X-ray of a person's thoughts. It's a report of an encounter. If you want to add material from elsewhere, there are conventions that determine how you should do that. If a person's words have been sufficiently transformed, they may no longer represent their point of view. An interview is reliant on this basic adherence to facts.

The other thing I did wrong was that several years ago I started to notice some things I didn't like in the Wikipedia entry about me, so I took them out. To do that, I created a user-name that wasn't my own. Using that user-name, I continued to edit my own Wikipedia entry and some other people's too. I took out nasty passages about people I admire. I factually corrected some other entries about other people. But in a few instances, I edited the entries of people I had clashed with in ways that were juvenile or malicious: I called one of them anti-Semitic and homophobic, and the other a drunk. I am mortified to have done this, because it breaches the most basic ethical standards. I apologise to the latter group unreservedly and totally. I am sorry.

But offering words of apology is not enough. In my work, I've spent a lot of time dragging other people's errors into the light. I did it because I believed that when you point out where somebody has gone wrong, you give them a chance to get it right next time. That's why, although it has been a painful process, and will surely continue to be, I think in the end I'll be grateful that my mistakes have been exposed in this way. I know that some of you have lost faith in me. I hope, after a period of absence, that you will give me another chance, while also remembering that copying is, at the zero level, a means of giving ideas a wider circulation. It's a valuable service that has been brought into disrepute by a culture that sanctifies ownership and commercial gain.

1. Non-sequiturs are a semi-reliable method of discouraging plagiarism. You have inserted one page of your own into these works, and think you just gave away which one it is . . . Actually it's the second time you've done it. Here you seek to expand on your theme, using the common device of a list of comparisons. (You'll return to those later). The idea is that you cannot resist including some of your own writing, which is so bad that it proves you could not have written the rest. (The ego is exposed, a spider on the gyroscope: rather than reproducing the text wholesale and remaining invisible, you were unable to resist making the change that bears your unmistakable marking).

4–5. The oiled wool sweaters manufactured (e.g. in Norway) for use by fisherman, skiers etc., and supposed to be damp-resistant, were usually made of wool which had not had the natural grease (forming about 40% of its bulk) washed out of it, as is normally done (and as was done in the ancient world), either before or after shearing, with the aid of soap. Nowadays the application of oil to synthetic fibres is a process sometimes used to make garments damp-resistant. One hardly need point out the appeal of such a garment to the artistic urban classes, keen to make an impression on their acquaintances, especially when one considers the addition of a hood. My version is defended from infringements by virtue of its quantity of errors, all easily detectable by the manufacturer. The origins of these garments are disguised and much disputed. In the ancient world, bards were considered sacred, and hoods may have been worn by them as ceremonial garb, or by pilgrims visiting certain cultural sanctuaries; but here we are on shaky ground, especially if we suggest the colour, uniformly grey or black, has any significance arising from those contexts. However, one can easily imagine the effect of a single hooded figure striding among the exotic and extravagant garments visible on the high street, their striking hues achieved by dyeing the fabrics first violet, then purple.

6. The effect is like that of a brick thrown through a window.

7f. The brick becomes a bird; it's notable how the bird is compared in turn to its reflection before hitting the glass, the 'hastening white wings' to the 'animated shadow' that rushes to meet it, representing its death on impact. The cracked or shattered window then creates multitudinous reflections of the bird, all of them 'dead versions'. It is debatable how to interpret the literary analogy, as it seems to reverse the conceit: the disguised page now appears to stand behind the 'real' bird, while the 'insubstantial hundred others' must correspond to the surrounding poems. Depending on whose authority you enlist, this entry is either an unwelcome imposter or the sole authentic inclusion in the book. As it appears among poems that necessarily predate it, one assumes that the disruptive power it produces in their ranks is emphasised, where it recasts the cohesive whole as an assortment of individual parts: beaks, bones and wings.

9. The dead bird's reflections stir and rise as 'many-toned nightingales / the wrecked street their sacred wood'. Whether their song mocks or memorialises their 'fallen' original (in the sense that the dead bird is doubly responsible for these newly activated images) is again ambiguous. It is traditionally the victims of violence who are transformed into nightingales, perhaps raising the possibility that the bird's death is in some way a consequence of its 'singing' (in the sense of an informant, one unable to keep a secret). In any case its silence is praised.

12. Tied to a brick or clutched in a dead bird's claws, the page is revealed to carry a 'conventional insult'.

[54]

If there are any still to be clinically loved
leave them here
on the bedside table
I have friends for that
but one remains I will not take
not here
among all these new acquaintances
look how old they are
in real life
and look at what they've prepared
in private
for their special friends

[55]

If you want to know my wishes briefly Mark,
famous host, bright ornament, ok then, pronto –
I ask to be the master of a great rural cultivator
of the soil, a small tribe used to the easiness of dirt.
I do. And to worship the cold painted rocks at dawn
with an unfit 'hello'. And later when the presents
are in stockings crowded by the chimney breast,
to remember the lead-haired fisherman I was then,
waiting a year for the prize of a red honey jar,
at a sagging table eating my eggs among ashes –
whoever does not love this does not love this life!
I hope that you live, and the city, amid duties.

[56]

Continually harassed wet vintage drips:
  you cannot, as I desire to, sell to the bishop, who is a mare.

[57]

What kind of life is called a healthy life . . . ?

I don't ask that it's too easy or too hard.

I'd like something in-between the two . . .

At the same time I don't want to know,

Even if it is my call . . . I know you know

I don't wish to shave my head again

Or work the funerals . . . the centre of attention . . .

At the same time I don't want to be bored!

Underneath the veil . . . in gloves and pearls . . .

W/r/t life . . . that's my prerogative . . . bitches . . .

[58]

What am I in spirit, Phoebus, but an average-sized dick: very early in the morning I approach the home of my friend, the wealthy older statesman who has expressed interest in the rhetorical style I'm polishing; I announce myself at his threshold with a scroll containing a hastily written panegyric – an offworld fantasy, pretty unfinessed – bulging my satchel. My bicycle is covered with notes for a thesis. As I'm waiting, smelling of nothing, I notice a bust of a non-figurative blue head in the lobby, quite powerful – and beyond it an animated painting with two identical caves in the background, each foretelling fortune (if you enter the correct one, you'll find yourself driving through a city with transparent walls), as well as several other mid-tech distractions. Eventually my tribute gains me access to the boardroom, where I face down two other candidates with a pitch on genres due for resurgence, and which, unless I misread his expression in the dawn shadows leaning through the room, appeals greatly to my prospective patron – this proposal I hold out with my stylus – engorged by the long delay – on the brink of convincing you, via a chubby portfolio – and afraid now of committing a solecism – that the human behind it is large.

[59]

Among tens of striplights shoaled
the dole,
the paucity of work experience
an obedience,
for an hour in a gloomy bath
the maths,
that all bets are flaccid wishes
warm washes,

[60]

Spacious though grim, rabbit. However
It's empty. I feel like a tooth.
The fall in the back and shoulders,
Inside I'm rotting. Tall
Felled wounded plant –
'Informal upright'. Same, mate.
Er you're not meant to pick them –
Teeth, blossoms, whatever.
Make a necklace.

[61]

Love's syllables scroll.
Tag them, Verona.
May is a happy man.
Consider pressed his tiny region.
Place the stars or less.
Fragrant hues applaud the Nile.
One tree sounds.
Love, the two unique dogs.
He speaks fluent hearts.
A dog can enjoy his humorous letter.
No one has bought cilantro, my arse.
Your lie, my boast.
I will not keep silent in the lawsuit, Bilbo.

[62]

'Penelope in the boardroom, Helen in the bedroom'. That's what they said about Laevinya Metelli. She had returned to her chambers late in the morning, where she was greeted by ardent birdsong and delirious lighting mimicking a stirring woodland. She had been riding and she stunk of horse. Pausing by the mirror to let her traditional hunting cloak slip from her shoulders, she looked out again over the resort: more than twenty square miles of upscaled terraforming, the latest in franchise vacationing. Beyond the garish greenery of the countryside pursuit zones, she could make out volcanic crusts of Martian rock, grey and mauve, through the vaporous haze from the thermal baths sunk into artificial terraces, rising at the settlement's perimeter. Somewhere down there, out of sight, was the vast crater, the so-called Delta of Venus, where the shrine in which she had invested so much energy, planning and fundraising, finally stood – stone and bronze in the alien atmosphere. She would see it tonight at last, for the opening sacrifice, her first time outside the domes. The sheer, anti-glare surfaces that encased the settlement for the most part preserved the illusion that the dark, rose-coloured sky hung above unroofed, and provided her now with the view that gave the sector its famous appeal. In the magnified upper-right quadrant of Laevinya's window, the earth hung like a bewitched apple, bright against its plush backdrop, with the white curve of the moon just visible beyond it – the next fruit, out of reach along a shady bough. Keeping her gaze on its unchanging glow, she eased her jodhpurs and transparent underwear down over her hips. Marcella would not be finished at the forum until after lunch. Slowly, Laevinya lifted and parted her buttocks, pulling them up and apart, and then letting them drop, feeling them bounce together, slapping them loudly with both upheld palms. She braced an index finger in the crease below each cheek, and coaxed the flesh into quick ripples, turning to observe the effect in the glass. A muted whistle of respiration disturbed her. She checked the mirror: Erotion was still in her bed, the sweep of his straight orange hair lying limply on the pillow. In their newly slaveless society, he was a member of the 'servant caste' or 's-caste', raised from birth to ameliorate the lifestyles of his masters – or rather, *clients*. The whistle of his breathing was produced by the valve surgically fitted in his windpipe: the sort of specialist touch the resort prided itself on. He had been added to the suite's list of accoutrements last night, on a whim, for a modest extra charge, when Laevinya decided she had tired of the luxury Centurion model included as the rental standard. Something between and inclusive of an exercise bike, pleasurebot, virtual reality set and film studio, the infinitely adaptable Centurions had revolutionised the erotic pastimes of all-female nobility, or 'purple-born' as they were colloquially known, not only catering, with almost excessive sensitivity and ingenuity, for any sexual impulse or sustained fantasy, however lavishly detailed or nuanced, but, if wished, enabling the experience to be simultaneous shared and expertly ornamented by the user's select network of co-fantasists. Occasionally though, such as on the previous evening, the body of a male subservient was required by Laevinya's highly tuned eros-complex. Erotion was not linguistic: that part of his brain had been burned out with medical instruments as an infant. On the dresser lay a small, rounded device, capable of programming and issuing instructions as visual cues, if the user desired. Laevinya had left the command cache empty, preferring to rely on the device's central, advertised function. She picked it up, and after a moment's reflection pressed the nub-like trigger on the handle and held it down. Just enough to wake him. There was an almost inaudible click, as a magnetised ball bearing moved into place over the tiny valve implanted in Erotion's windpipe, cutting off the air flow. The whistling stopped. When the body on the bed jerked into consciousness, Laevinya released the nub-like trigger, keeping the device in her palm, and stood at the mirrored dresser with her back to the bed. A lifetime of calculated guesswork had honed the s-caste's attention to a preternatural level, making him able to intuit his client's current wish and to anticipate their next, almost before it was thought. Laevinya heard him move swiftly over the bedclothes until his face was level with her rear. He let out a murmur of gratitude as she bent her spine to reveal her anus and pressed it against his waiting mouth. Erotion's tongue, a muscle with the sole purpose of providing stimulation, adapted fluently to its task: agile and flickering, it hovered and delved, activating a nest of nerve-endings. At unpredictable intervals she squeezed the nub-like trigger on the device's handle, cutting off his oxygen, causing the investigative flurries to intensify and deepen.

She pulled open her riding blouse to expose her breasts, the nipples hardened to antennae-like points, and returned her gaze to the distant planet in the window, her sudden and superb indifference for it somehow mixing with her pleasure. She moved backwards, pushing her buttocks more firmly into the s-caste's face, the bridge of his nose squashing against the base of her spine. Almost kneeling now, she relaxed her thighs, allowing his head and neck to take her entire weight; without breaking contact Erotion moved backwards and efficiently lowered onto the bed to accommodate her more fully. The articulate darting of his tongue and lips had streamlined into rhythmical thrusting and sucking. A vision took over as Laevinya stared, hypnotised, on the tattered drapes of cloud that swaddled the earth, as they seemed to swirl in real time, hiding the imperial blue of the seas from sight, passing in great sweeps like warflags in semaphore, then colliding and boiling, dissipating into steam, so when they cleared, she realised with excitement, there was nothing there, only the vacancy of space, the fruit had fallen, the bough was bare . . . She released a long, controlled sigh that held a short, low cry at its centre, and circled her hips, seeking rigidity, a point of resistance in the wetness beneath her. She looked down: her finger was clasped, bone-white, on the device's trigger. To her right she could see the fingers of Erotion's hand, stiffened and trembling. The skin on his wrist, as with all s-castes, was so pale it was translucent: she watched the tight veins as they ticked with blood. At length, she lifted herself from her fully seated position, only then releasing the device from her grasp. Nothing – but after a second, a gargle came from the bed, like a bathtub draining. Oh well. Marcella would complain about the bill. Laevinya glanced down to the gravel paths that gridded the walled garden directly below her window, half-expecting to see her now, striding towards their quarters in her formal grey cloak, pleased to be back, asking about lunch.

But it was still too early. Laevinya stretched, raising her arms above her head, and chose a white gown from the wardrobe, a high neckline and a severe cut, hanging it by the dresser. Very Penelope, she thought, smiling. She finished undressing briskly and stepped into the washroom, which immediately lit up and hummed. Phew. After the morning she'd had, it wasn't surprising she needed to shower. She was almost getting hungry, too. As the first perfectly chilled jet of water touched her brow, her already distant thought of planetary destruction began to evaporate, and a second later it had vanished completely.

[63]

In general I hate discussing my poetry
so I always ask questions
there's a kind of writer/artist though
and you meet them all the time now
who only talks about their 'practice'
without anyone caring or asking
(it isn't connected to success)
and shows no flicker of interest
in anything anyone else does
if the choice is between talking about me
when I don't want to talk about me
or talking about you
when you only want to talk about you
then let's talk about me
by the way if you don't know
this type of artist you probably are it sorry

[64]

I want to use the line 'the rich are never beautiful' because to me it sounds believable. It sounds believable when I walk through Knightsbridge, as I occasionally have had to, and see the fabulous people going in and out of the gourmet pie shops, going in and out of Zara and Chanel, clutching small black objects that from here could be sunglasses or could be networking devices, some of them famous from structured-reality TV shows, some of them known for being no-platformed by London universities, one of them famous for being Gok Wan – most of them not famous or known at all, really, but attempting to simulate a certain sort of frictionless carapace as they part the throngs of people milling on the sunlit streets. One of them says 'When in NW1' loudly into a phone. As I finish my Happy Meal I have to concede that a few of them are genuinely hot, though.

1. The point the poem seems to be making is that one is less beautiful when one tries to enhance one's beauty or when one invites appreciation of it, but frankly this position is much too fraught with issues around patriarchal standards, conventional heterosexual expectations and conformity to gender ideals, for someone like me to weigh in on, really, other than to signal my wary distance from it. Trying to be as honest as I can be, I guess the only type of beauty that I am reliably attracted to I would probably term 'post-hot.' [Insert image of a non-descript stretch of water.]
3–4. The name 'Fabulla', given to the vain young woman in the poem (here infelicitously rendered as 'fabulous'), may well have been selected due to its proximity to *fabula*, or 'fable'. Whether or not the reader chooses to hear this as an offensive stereotype, or as a comment on the artifice of Fabulla's presentation as comparable to the arguably more cynical fabrications of the poet's own micro-managed appearance, probably comes down to their proclivity for over-interpretation and their wavering or already-routed sympathy with the material thus far. Still with me?
12. Free machine translation repeatedly suggests 'recipe' for *fabula*, raising the possibility of a more problematic version, like maybe a poem in ugly prose that instructs the cast of *Made in Chelsea* to fuck, slaughter, prep, cook and devour each other in a televised Bacchanalian orgy-type event-ordeal / fixed-

rig cookery contest cross-over / season finale. The host (me) bastes himself while turned on a spit.

[65]

When I say 'tree', laughing as foreign words
may be called 'figs', the blind, you say,
say 'the fig tree', which we know to be born in a tree,
but we say 'figs', the blind, the LORD.
When I say the 'wood' laughs, for the debts of figs
said to the fig-tree, the blind, you say,
the fig tree, shall we say, we know to be born in a tree,
we figs, blind.
When I say 'timber', laughing, the debts of figs
blind you to the tree,
the fig tree, we know we will be born in a tree.
Figs are blind.
When I say 'timber', laughing, the debts of figs
are blind to the tree,
we know to be born in a tree of the fig tree.
Tree blind.
When I say 'the wood', a laugh, very much in the air,
is blind to the tree,
we are born in a tree tree.
Wood blind.
When I say of the trees, the laughter of the air, for the most part,
blind into a tree,
we are born in a tree.
Wood blind.
When I say, for the most part of the air, the laughter of the trees,

blind in a tree.
We are born into a tree.
Wood blind.
If I say, of the air, for the most part, the laughter of the trees,
a blind man in a tree.
We are born into a tree.
Wood blind.

FRIENDSHIP, FAMILY, MARRIAGE

[66]

I Wrote It for You and *A Novel By* are possible titles of the unpublished novel James Gillespie leaves on his PC to be discovered by his girlfriend, played by Samantha Morton, after he kills himself. I'm not sure we are ever made aware of the method of his suicide, but it is certainly violent. It's coming up to Christmas and the multi-coloured lights on the small tree in the hallway pulse above his bloodied corpse: perhaps he anticipated this and the ghoulishness of the scene appealed to him. Gillespie's note begins with the blunt imperative *READ THIS* (another title?) which is typed on the first page of the document containing his novel. He provides little explanation for his actions, only commenting that it 'felt like the right thing to do', which sounds too much like an excuse provided after the fact, almost as if his spirit were actually communicating via the flashing cursor at the start of his message (an authorial touch: he edited). Apart from a brief mention of money held in a savings account, the short note is devoted to plans for the novel, with instructions to send the manuscript to several London publishers, which he lists in order of preference. At first glance, the ambition of Gillespie's gambit seems impressive, if somewhat adolescent in its energy: death in this life, for immortality in literature. The author of a singular work, written in obscurity, *felled by his own hand* – there's an urgency to his bid for posthumous fame that verges on neediness, and which could be touching or gauche or both, finally the presumption is irritating though, a response that we sense Samantha Morton will arrive at too, even as she numbs herself at a party with booze and pills in the wake of the tragedy, keeping the news to herself. As well as the novel, he leaves a number of other gifts, wrapped up like Christmas presents (are they still Christmas presents, functionally speaking?); these items are narcissistic in scope and add a cinematic flourish to his already theatrical exit. A leather jacket, brand new. A Walkman. A mixtape (*Music For You*, another title, he can't help it). A cigarette lighter in a special leather case. Maybe a pair of aviator sunglasses, but I could have made those up; anyway it's as if he is asking the recipient to live inside a late album by the Cure. Selecting these purchases, wrapping them in tone-deaf patterned paper, Gillespie undoubtedly imagined Samantha Morton ghosting the high street in a gothic aura they'd make potent: a figure in an immaculate leather jacket, smoking a cigarette, listening on headphones to the soundtrack he made for the movie she is in. Here she sits on a swing in a deserted playground; here she stands near the sea at dusk, with mauve clouds, blank to it all: is that what we're watching? Imagining these scenes makes us confront Gillespie's determination to author and licence his girlfriend's grief from a point beyond death. You sense that for him these images possess a power he believes will ensure their permanence, that Samantha Morton's funereal outline will endlessly circuit the bars, the shops, the cemetery, the plume from her cigarette forming his signature; that her taciturn affairs will be morbid recreations of their relationship, unable to survive in the strained daylight that characterises her waking life; that the blue horizon will seal at head-height with the level weight of his genius. He must have felt very certain of her temperament: a novelist's certainty. It's important that we detect from the outset Samantha Morton's resistance to the role that her character's dead boyfriend has prepared for her: even as she reads his note for the first time, her features, unearthly pale (as Gillespie might put it) in the dreary light from the monitor, disclose a faint scepticism. The note is unconvincing for a few reasons

I've already hinted at. Later, we see her appraise the document at greater length: *I wrote it for you*. The novel's female narrator, described by the publisher as 'a distinctive and original voice', informs us why it has no title. As she deletes her boyfriend, letter by letter and, letter by letter, spells out herself, we witness something that's seldom recorded: the displacement of a name from subject to author, as effortless and ingenious as tearing out a page. You sense the act's peculiar finality. Her ascension from the epigraph she embodied a moment ago (desultory, passive: a dedication) invites the total collapse of the fiction's economy; when Samantha Morton hits print, her book becomes the receipt all writing is: an obliterated name, a payment deposited. Or, to put it another way, revenge is served. She is associated with a scribble on a strong six-figure cheque. Samantha Morton is never seen to read the novel, and her disinterest, expressed eloquently in her decision to go immediately to Spain and do loads of MDMA, shows us the only interpretation left: that she doesn't need to, that is, that this note is just the preface, that I am necessarily a fantasy, a literary device resembling a person, and she had to climb inside my name, to dismantle it from within, dance on my remains, and so ensure my silence. Samantha Morton reappears as a legal function at the other end of a terracotta corridor, holding an identical red flower; like her holiday, the rest is fiction.

[67]

Basically my critics fall into two categories: those who think I 'go too far' and those who think I 'don't go far enough'. The first group are literal minded conservatives who routinely confuse innovation with novelty; fundamentally conformist, with a fervour for accessibility, they over-identify with tradition as a benchmark of literary achievement. They want their poetry tastefully tinted by the contemporary, not determined by it; this leads them to praise nostalgia as the foremost 'poetic feeling'; they favour the elegy. The latter are conventional minded radicals who routinely mistake referencing for criticality; fundamentally contrarian, with a fondness for hyperbole, they over-identify with rebellion as the index of literary ambition, as they might put it, *par excellence*. They want their poetry uneasily inflected by its inheritance, not enslaved by it. This leads them to praise abjection as the foremost 'poetic affect'; they too favour the elegy. We should ask both sides the same question: 'if poetry in its current forms was wiped out tomorrow, couldn't we hope it was replaced with something better?', and dismiss them with the same premise: there are two types of people, and people who get it.

[68]

Rufus is such a sad dude. Poor Rufus! Whatever he's doing, he only thinks about Neve. It's actually pretty boring. If he's happy (which is rare) he talks about something supposedly funny she did, and if he's sad and silent (as usual) you can be sure he's thinking of her. Whenever you see him he normally he ends up crying. Thing is, he's never actually met Neve: she died about 200 years before he was born. He has thousands of pictures, a lot of them stuck up on a wall in his house, like a shrine almost. It's creepy. And some of the pictures are not of Neve at all, but of women that, let's say, approximate a certain 'Neve-ness' in their expression or attire. Neve died before there was technology to produce a convincing post-life avatar, which is probably a good thing. You sense that if Neve were to reappear, even as a simulation, it would trigger some kind of crisis in Rufus's personality. He's become basically the salesman of his sadness. It's totally his brand. He wrote all those songs, and people love how *into* Neve he is, despite the total impossibility of it and everything. Actually, I get the feeling that if the real Neve, or her modern-day equivalent, Neve-II, walked into one of his shows, he wouldn't even look up from his keyboard. It's really dumb.

[69]

poem addressed to parents
poem paying tribute to family pets
poem drawing attention to dry and damaged hair
poem reporting the bad behaviour of a friend
poem rhapsodising the evaporation of dew
poem warning of consequences of non-payment
poem boasting about oral technique
poem chastising large appetites
poem demonstrating silence
poem on the dangers of drinking
poem on the uses of deities
poem addressed to deities
poem paying tribute to drinking
poem drawing attention to silence
poem admiring large appetites
poem reporting oral technique

poem rhapsodising the consequences of non-payment
poem warning of the evaporation of dew
poem boasting about the bad behaviour of a friend
poem demonstrating dry and damaged hair
poem on the dangers of family pets
poem on the uses of parents

[70]

[. . .] go there on my behalf, bearing these words in print,
Glossy and respectful before all types of household
  intelligence.
Again, I should add. And find near the edge of theory
A path through virginal snow at the outskirts of your home
That leads you to the wide lake you recognise from dreams
Where your supreme leader's image shines upon the water,
Not restraining the wonderful radiance of her complexion;
She rejoices in your praise which is nowadays considered
To overcome the size of the work and be discernible both
  below
And beyond it, a trend like that in which the rivers and roads
Are covered with wet reflections of the surrounding world,
Proving that (behold) before dome stands dome stands dome,
Visible even from your window as a kind of shining approach
And for this reason you needn't fear the glare of its proud
  threshold,
Which means nothing more than the gatepost means to the
  house
And is no nearer to her than the attitudes of her imperious
  sisters,
And if they ask you why you came, you will be armed with
  an excuse:

I came for these poems, these things, that I could not have written [. . .]

[71]

While working on this section of the book I was experiencing some difficulties with my marriage. My wife and I had slept apart for four or five nights following what should have been an inconsequential argument; at the same time I had begun reading *Contempt* by Alberto Moravia, a novel about a man who starts to suspect that his wife no longer loves him. As I was reading the book in the bath one evening, the scenes it described, somewhat recognisable to me at that moment, began to take on the disturbing, external life of premonitions. This was a sensation that, as I experienced it, I could dimly recall having in previous relationships – a novel or film entering my awareness, revealing my situation in a new light and even seeming to predict how events would unfold. As I progressed quickly though the first two or three chapters, I saw that my own experience might easily proceed on a kind of parallel track to the drama of the novel, and I could picture specific and equivalent future scenes which had the clarity of recent memories. Normally, imagining some disaster befalling me or my loved ones carries with it a peculiar reassurance, as if by reasoning through such things deliberately I could somehow discount them from the range of outcomes – as if I could charm them out of plausibility – detailing them in my imagination, and in doing so removing them safely to a fictional order of reality. But this time the ritual failed to work convincingly; instead, the forecast of the novel began to appear all the more inevitable, and, far from warding off such a future, my daydreaming seemed in fact to be attracting its currents towards me. By now I had stopped reading and was gazing at the bulging reflections in a misted, metallic part of the shower fitting. But I was unable to disengage myself from the procedures of the story – I felt powerless, certain that events had already progressed too far along this line of development to be reversed, that I had become committed to their sequence, as one commits to an argument, developing it step by step, until you find yourself at a point so distant it seems unconnected to your original impulse. Although my surroundings were completely familiar, it was as though I had looked up to find myself in another room entirely. And yet I was also aware that this space, like a newly remembered life – where my wife and I not only no longer felt any affection towards each other, but actively behaved as if the other didn't exist – had been present during every moment of our relationship, like a basement below the rooms we lived in, that I had now managed to knock a hole or passage into, through simple disregard or negligence. The previous night, in a morbid mood, I had looked up, one by one, each of my significant exes. Now, through the opening I had made, and from which it seemed blew a stale breeze, I was able to watch certain scenes culminate before me. I observed a hasty reunion with an old girlfriend, who I had discovered was recently divorced, and felt the passing glow of a particularly shabby sort of happiness in the wake of having slept with her again – even the subdued buzz of anticipation as I debated whether or not to text or email her over the following couple of days. Any excitement was quickly dispersed, leaving behind it the unmistakable contours of a long-term solitary existence: as I considered it, it seemed I already inhabited its outline, and that all that was required to bring it into focus was a small shift of emphasis in my self-regard. I sensed the brittleness of my personality becoming tougher, more resistant, my confidence diminishing to a rudimentary defensiveness, I saw the furnishings that would come to witness most of my activities. I felt unsure at that moment if I rose from the bath and stepped into the hallway I wouldn't find myself in the new life I had just imagined into being – it had grown in brightness and clarity and now, by some alchemical magic, it was threatening to obscure my old life altogether. It was beyond doubt, I felt, that I had assisted this destructive vision in reaching its position of dominance. Not by allowing it to take shape in my consciousness over the last fifteen or twenty minutes, as I lay in the bath, but, surely, over a period of years – gradually and by increments I had been collecting the materials of this competing reality: silences from arguments and moments of cold introspection, and I had been storing away these elements, like rare powders necessary to produce pigments of unusual density and strength. The thought that came to me next was of the irritation and bemusement I had observed between ex-spouses – an attitude of confusion and annoyance rather than anger – because the shared image of their relationship had been corrupted somehow without either of them intending it; they had permitted the ascendency of an image, until the effects of its prominence, like dark rays that permeated all corners of life, could no longer be averted. The swiftness of the reversal was possible due to this latent material, abundant and instantly accessible (stored in canisters in some back-end facility, as I visualised it, a rich ink beyond black, of perfect consistency). This was the cause of the image's troubling proximity, only a moment away, the click of a door coming-to, an arm's reach into another room. I rose from the bath and pulled out the plug. I felt I had achieved some measure of control over the novel's unsettling effect on me; still, it was necessary to safeguard myself against its influence – wrapped in a towel on the edge of the bed, I noted down my thoughts as best I could, in my anxiety first selecting a notebook that didn't contain any autobiographical writing, such was my fear that committing these impressions to paper could contaminate other areas of my life (anxious also that in neglecting my real-life problems I was in further danger of condemning myself to the fate of Moravia's narrator). As I tried to remember the order in which my thoughts had occurred to me, I re-experienced the vertiginous sensation of reading the novel's opening pages, but at a much reduced intensity. Concerned now with recording the feeling as accurately as possible, I already found myself less occupied with the intrusion itself than with the methods available to me in copying it down. I began to write, all the time becoming more removed from the experience – I felt as though it were being safely contained, packaged in a durable box whose fibres were the sentences that described its now-hidden contents. I was succeeding, it seemed, in eliminating it – the effort of putting it down in writing worked very much like the charm of imagining a misfortune in order to discount it – encasing it in a style no doubt cribbed from the novel I had just been reading, and relegating it to a discrete conceptual space. Even referring to my wife as 'my wife', as I did in the second sentence I had written, transformed the events into events in the life of a total stranger – a remote, notional figure, sewn in a world of colourless routines. That night, I had the latest in a series of dreams set in a half-familiar city. As I walked I could see its districts climbing the hillsides, whole areas that for some reason had become derelict. This expanse of empty streets that ringed the town was in the process of being destroyed, yet some of the houses were still used, secretively and spontaneously, many containing stores of food and building materials, and somehow it was clear to me that these supplies were intended as offerings to the dead. Other houses were more or less intact as homes, with the dusty artefacts of their ex-inhabitants, blankets and chess-sets and kettles – these could be used safely for a night or two. Still others contained sophisticated traps. The dead were present throughout the district, not visibly, but archived inside the houses; in this sense, as well as in its silence, the zone resembled a library. In the dream, the notes I had taken after reading the start of Moravia's novel had become mixed up with tributes left in the abandoned homes – later it turned out that my wife had found them (a large, untidy bundle of papers in the dream) and, having read them, consigned them to one of the makeshift shrines. In the dream, I entered this area designated for the dead in order to retrieve them. When I woke, slightly feverish, so early it was hardly light, my first thought was of the notes I had written the night before; my fear was that my wife had discovered them and would perhaps misinterpret them, in view of our ongoing domestic stalemate, as revealing a desire to dissolve the marriage. Then a new thought followed, which seemed in the grey light that fanned from above the curtains into the spare bedroom startlingly clear to me. In a world in which the dead are archived, an account, such as the one I had written, would serve as a means of locating a specific individual, a self among the archived selves: it would be used like a set of directions to identify a strand of consciousness among all the accumulated consciousnesses stored in the vast repositories of the dead. This explained the overwhelming sense I had had of *answering a description* when beginning to read Moravia's novel – in a way it was a call, a *command*. And in order to distinguish myself from its search, it was required (it seemed clear at that moment) that I produce a piece of writing which provided the true details of my passage through the archive, and marked it as distinct – and so I decided to write down these observations, too, in the hope of succeeding in my intention.

[72]

The authors on my bookshelves include Chekhov, Kierkegaard, de Sade, Mishima, Joyce, Ellison, Kesey. Archive footage from the 1960s plays outside my window constantly: fuzzy events trembling on the world stage, moonlit basketball games, stuff like that. I am a reclusive older writer played by Sean Connery – 'Salingeresque' – and one night my apartment is broken into by a group of black teenagers who, looking for a stereo or television, steal a few of my more select volumes. When I catch them in the act they disperse like silverfish across my dim kitchen, the fleetest member of the crew dropping a grey Jansport backpack as he makes good his escape – that was you – another muttering something I hear as, 'Ever see a ghost that wasn't white?' – presumably referring to my spectral appearance at the scene. In the backpack I discover your notebooks, which I decide to annotate and return, adding these comments in red pen: 'unworthy of the reader', 'constipated thinking', 'this passage fantastic', 'specificity', 'atmosphere pungent', 'constipated' (again), 'where are you taking me?' and, 'Stay the fuck out of my home'. I set you homework. Bright saxophones blowse – yes, blowse – through my time-speckled windows: tonight I'm drinking. Nursing these fantasies of having a protégé. In the morning, the footage outside has switched to nature documentaries, and I'm birdwatching peacefully – 'An adult male, quite pretty!' – but what am I suggesting? I came to Brooklyn in my late teens and I understand e v e r y t h i n g about white imperialism. Something to do with Nazis and the BMW propeller symbol. I always hope someone will ask if I've read all the books that line the walls, and I like to give advice – 'no thinking'. I seem to view writing principally as a physical activity. Picture me outside a cabin, chopping wood, my epic clouds of breath: that's the blueprint. I go so far as to describe the typewriter as a musical instrument, and I have some other opinions. 'Really punch the keys!' I advise. 'You've got rhythm!' When you are disgraced by your professor in retaliation for getting smart, I start to view you as the conduit in a relationship between two elderly male academics. A little bit. I took the bell out of my phone, so why would I give you the number? Why is everything in black and white again? Then, an accusation: you plagiarised my short story, which has the risible title – I almost can't bring myself to type it – 'A season of faith's perfection'. The consensus is that either you have an uncommon gift. Or. Automatic writing? Eidetic memory? When you ask for my help I become angry (my weakness is that I'm quick to anger) – actually I have deep-seated agoraphobia and haven't left my apartment in years. You have a history of people not telling you, and should be redeemed by sport, with a bit of luck. All that stuff about what I'm really trying to say, I finally fluffed it. Nothing there. So instead I read aloud your work in front of them, but I don't tell them it's your work, or I only tell them it at the end. They're taken aback, massively, by the big reveal – stunned murmurs, many hands unclasping at once – so your work must sound a lot like my work, perhaps. The whole thing is in this weird fog, a fading montage, where everyone holds a self-consciously rapt expression. Your Sunday prose. One line stands out: 'having family obliges us to find new family', which makes no sense, Erotion. And then I'm dead, and you're writing the foreword to my only famous novel, my famous only novel, and the footage is of helicopters now, in colour, herding us into the future, presumably, or quite possibly bearing my coffin, which is called *Sunset*.

[73]

Once nobody in town would touch it
A forbidden precinct of expression
Now the disembodied are attracted to the power vacuum
There are spirits in the kiosk
Rich friends with dark opinions, suspicious of the boycott
In sepulchral apartments their views sound placid
Inspiring individual awe for a public necrology
Its heavy garland flowers a dream world
Watching lightning striding up the Thames
In a description of the present, or the actual present
And we were protected by a sort of baroque realism
The crowd that fucks with us is a clever man

[74]

She says
that when
she says
she's married

a red
fedora
appears
on her head

[75]

. . . I don't believe anything

I half-believe everything . . .

[76]

—Oh my cares, my money is worthless.
'I'd be doing it anyway'
(So goes the hopeful cry from inside the festival.)
correlation of low income with happiness
Defer the songs-and-dances that answer it,
the vagaries of fortune; intergenerational wealth
your subscribers don't pay you anything. (We gave out deals to those
content is free for the readers that count
people.) What did you expect while you snoozed—an advance?
correlation of work ethic with success
Generally artists are grasping and selfish (Correction: ambitious
morals of the hustle
and individualistic.) The title you're wreathed in can't compensate you.
authenticity isn't comforting
Over in gallery districts, money trees bend to their variegated load.
fees, travel opportunities, etc.
Magazines offer tap water and chilly integrity, 'everything's political',
e.g. panels at book festivals

And the sound of someone somewhere enjoying an hors
d'oeuvre.

the appreciative audience

What has it got to do with you, anyway? (Suggestion: or is
no one

no one's immune

immune?) Curious, the market floats closer, its scenes reflected

supply chains for creative economies

as in a bubble of soap. The chairs at the readings refuse to
kiss asses.

the lure of populism, novelty

(Translation: accept the loose change.) You can hear a dream
pop.

selling out

Late one Friday night in early November, Jun Rekimoto, a distinguished professor of human–computer interaction at the University of Tokyo, was online preparing for a lecture when he began to notice some peculiar posts rolling in on social media . . . So begins the article in *The New York Times* that my dad forwarded me in January. I can't seem to read it all the way through, though. Digested read: Google Translate has radically improved due to applications from AI technology. Using a process known as statistical machine translation, Google Translate finds recurring patterns in large volumes of translated material, and extracts these rules to produce its translations, rather than learning all the grammatical intricacies of a given language. Google is obviously an ideological apparatus, intent on total coverage through its particular filter, with English as the 'neutral setting' where all other languages are forced to rendezvous.

Oh my cares, my money is worthless,
O care not to cheapen the price of my Health
o for me their price is not meanness into my hands

to ask questions, hope and child's home,
hope and child abroad differ
hope and homeless alumni,

goes different singing and dancing sisters;
singing and dancing sisters;
postpone incantations

brass, Damsel, I give out of those men to be.
brass, Damsel, I give out of those men to be
copper will give of these there is no girl for you.

What do you ask of a doze? Genius has a money box;
What do you ask of a doze? Genius has a money box;
what you are looking for? His money box spinning;

The more a phrase is found in the vast corpora of text available, the more it will be offered as translation – as a dead language Latin doesn't fare particularly well under these conditions. Until now, Google's interpretative pulses had failed to properly reanimate it, manufacturing instead a half-functioning approximation, a kind of zombie. In order to 'learn', an AI is effectively 'punished' when it submits an incorrect result: eventually it is shocked into realism. These improvements have compromised my activities, relying as they do on patchwriting outputs produced by Google Translate's attempts to turn Latin poetry into passable English, a process rich with pathos and ruinous comedy, indicating both the lossy edges of internet imperialism and the irretrievable distance of the source text. My wetware only works in that shrinking margin of error. If the translations become *too good*, I will have to resort to a more primitive online translator to simulate inaccuracy, defeating the programmatic aspect of the research – or I will have to start reproducing Google Translate's 'adequate' translations (in other words admitting defeat), a development I hadn't anticipated.

she is shrewd, one of the gods of these things, all his income.
she is shrewd, one of the gods of these things, all his income.
these tastes, these all lend one of the gods.

What can they give ivy? Pale tree
What can they give ivy? Pale tree
what can time be to give? Pall tree

inclines various weighted black hair.
inclines various weighted black hair.
tendency various the weight of the black hair.

in addition to the waters, and the garlands and the lyres of
the goddesses
garlands and the lyres of the goddesses
garlands and the lyres of the goddesses, and in addition to
drinking water,

and the great, and has no substance, but a matter of through
the void.
and in addition to all the woes of the waters, and the great thing,
but a matter of emptiness
nothing has and great, but a matter of the void.

As a small-scale web developer and early internet adopter, my dad loathes Google, and has even gone to the lengths of getting his home removed from Google Earth – you slide straight past his section of street, the address an elision or slippage. Part of his bitter antipathy towards the tech giant is due to the fact that much of his income depends on the leasing of an online calendar system he designed in the early 2000s to various low-involvement holiday-let interests. His fearful prediction is that it is only a matter of time before Google's appetite for expansion will cause them to supersede it with an, if not superior, then almost certainly more user-friendly, widely available and widely compatible alternative. This is information I remain more or less indifferent to, although I still primarily use a hotmail email address, an increasingly conspicuous anachronism.

What do you think? What with the naked permission?
What do you think? What with the naked permission?
what do you have? Why do we permit nakedness?

Deeper market is closer to the Roman gods.
Even the rich are closer to the Roman Forum
The Roman Forum is seriously late

there are struck by the air, but around our platforms
there the air sounds, but around the platforms
there the airs sound: around the stage

are the barren, and the seats of them that only smack of kisses.
and the seats of them that only smack of kisses.
and barren chairs where kisses alone rumble.

Through the hours he spends in his office, lit only by twin tropical fish tanks, my father has intimated that rather than relying on a reasonably steady income stream from a decade-old piece of code I can only dimly apprehend, I should make more concerted preparations for the future. I visit a voluble elderly relative at his house in Notting Hill to try and get an 'in' to the publishing industry, which he retired from more than a decade ago. In a room with tall, tasteful paintings and dark, decorative furniture, including a working grandfather clock, my great-uncle monologues comfortably, revealing over the course of a couple of hours that his success at a major London publishing house came at the cost of his marriage, his family, his happiness, etc. I have not heard of most of the people and companies he mentions. I do not read *The Bookseller*. I leave in some confusion; outside the streets of West London are bright and blurred in the August heat. The Google car goes past, capturing everything.

[77]

Sleeps late, still pale.
Sits up, still pale.
Starts pilates, still pale.
Spatial pull, still pale.
Sees poll, still pale.
Last lap, still pale.
Sublets apt., still pale.
Lies well, still pale.
Slaps stacks, still pale.
Sets up laptop, still pale.
Steeps tea, still pale.
Skips *install*, still pale.
Spells 'Psi', still pale.
Lifts pattern, still pale.
Styles palettes, still pale.
Taps caps, still pale.
Tapered slacks, still pale.
Art pact, still pale.
Oils pelt, still pale.
Staples pleats, still pale.
Sands sill, still pale.
Spins plates, still pale.
Collects petals, still pale.
Less ill, still pale.
Il s'appelle, still pale.
Spits spiel, still pale.
Leaves spa, still pale.
Sap sinks, still pale.
Passes salt, still pale.
Tests pastels, still pale.
Contracts STI, still pale.
Sips Lilt, still pale.

Pats tail, still pale.
Apes lapse, still pale.
Paints alps, still pale.
Slits sacks, still pale
Sifts lake, still pale.
Pans silt, still pale.
Smooths lapels, still pale.
Seals letter, still pale.
Steals fill, still pale.
Tastes stale, still pale.
Slates loss, still pale.
Pastes lists, still pale.
Slips bill, still pale.
Parallel parks, still pale.
Reads lips, still pale.
Lisps reply, still pale.
Selects all, still pale.
Tips least, still pale.
Seals pits, still pale.
Stalls cops, still pale.
Tills soil, still pale.
Makes plea, still pale.
Bells peal, still pale.
Leaps stile, still pale.
Casts pall, still pale.
Visits isle, still pale.
Tells walls, still pale.
Spills teal, still pale.
Swallows pill, still pale.
Repeats tale, still pale.
Pulls plaits, still pale.
Plies staff, still pale.
Piles tall, still pale.
Sells deal, still pale.

[78]

In the dream your weeping friends had dried your cheeks
having already gone for a last dip in the lake at Styg Fest
and you decided not to drink the familiar admixture
(though you were thirsty) but deserted them when they
weren't looking
into the woods some said shedding your clothing as you
walked
into the black waters some said floating with weeds and
garbage
or (some said) you disappeared backstage and never returned
in any case without saying anything you discreetly receded
which was the way you always chose to leave parties
wishing (but not too hard) you could hear them ask about
you
or know they'd return more fully to your side in conversation
as though to a single copy of something they'd all been read-
ing
and when they put down the worn book the report would be
(but we feel there's something missing from this chapter . . .)

[79]

With regards to causes, the objects are always doing something you do, but so is it always:
that is to say, it is not something they do, but rather that you are always doing something.
Through the whole business they are like a briefcase that's gone missing; mulishly, you're searching.
The nature of this is not exactly forthcoming, but it is something to do with the 'wounds of the soul'.

[80]

Time for my annual update. You may have been wondering
about my lack of presence lately. For your attention:
depressed and 37,
last night I admitted I need validation. I will fucking die this
year otherwise.
It has been requested, cos we're not even (not a threat just a
statement
of fact). Thanks in advance (there was that, but 80 isn't even
recognition).

– M.

LAW AND RHETORIC

[81–98]

This section originally appeared at the beginning of the book. The author's right to be identified has been asserted in accordance with Section 77 of the Copyright, Designs and Patents act 1988. First printed in England, perhaps during the campaign of 77–84 AD. A CIP record is available from the British Library. Composed by Marcus Valerius, and recovered by Erotion®, property of Google Inc. Lorem ipsum dolor sit amet, consectetur adipiscing elit. Soccer school textbooks, CNN in Canberra not, please Planning fears. Nutrition targeted only at id feugiat. Nutrition residents soccer sad old and ugly netus et malesuada hunger and poverty. Mid-afternoon, or at Laoreet players, members of the propaganda chili, developers need players smile a refund. Headlines region, which has been manufacturing football, receives as propaganda. Mauris dictum of the competition, nor any other. Fusce dictum, the price of the righteous, at times a great man, itself, the very expected, the of life, consectetur orci felis ac erat. In the region, Japan developer of carrots deductible is set. Japan core in the thermal live in ecological players sometimes. Curabitur blandit, there was no bow, viverra dignissim. No price sterilized lion, photography ultricies Reserved basketball yet. Maecenas hatred, an alarm clock or developers, members of any recipe. For which is the urna sapien. Microwave drink a lot of pot, or put pregnant outdoor volleyball. Android and the players. Mauris sed erat tristique, consectetur lacus ac, ullamcorper arcu. The kids cartoon cat, he graduated quiver biggest football. However, developers gas consumer, who skirt the arc Planning. There was nothing 'natural' about the death of Brittany Murphy, who was poisoned to death in 2012 by government spooks. She was under close surveillance after she spoke out in defence of Department of Homeland Security whistle-blower Julia Davis. Davis claims to have worked as a stunt double for Angelina Jolie, and believes she was under heavy surveillance by the government. Toxicology tests revealed heavy metal poisoning in Murphy's hair and tissue samples. Her husband Simon Monjack died 5 months later. The couple exhibited signs like headaches, dizziness, abdominal cramps, coughing, sweating, disorientation, wheezing, congestion and pneumonia. A great mourning in the ac lacus aliquam sit amet Suspendisse in lorem. Integer sit amet augue vitae augue tincidunt element. Nulla volutpat of peril from the, dignissim tincidunt nisl lobortis non. Clinical bananas may not need members. Microwave bananas mass before and sometimes sad. Of life, but diam nutrition fermentation. Film or tomato minutes or tomato sapien. The biggest Aliquam facilisis purus nec ligula hendrerit. In time to come, that the ends of the facilisis ligula drink. At the time, my television and bananas. Yes I told my friends quite literally that Brittany Murphy was murdered. I suspected it of Heath Ledger's death as well. Fit into this, Michael Jackson. Not to mention that if the cause of the two deaths was from toxic molds in the house I am sure that the previous owner Britney Spears would come forward about this possibility, plus one would think Spears would have warned them about the toxic mould in the house. Tomorrow targeted at customers. Gluten. Clinical for textbooks, Laoreet or carton and, developers and clinical. Now anyone or antioxidants. Till goodies. Present a lot of protein mass, but in Oklahoma. Aenean sit amet erat vel elit feugiat sit amet are not interested in the throat. Largest themed or things. However, they need vehicles sauce fermentation. However, it was but the eu. Homework has been arc diameter. During this time I was being gang stalked. I tried to tell Kamala Harris and I cried out to everyone I knew, even the FBI with my computer hack evidence. No one helped me. I risk my life by this statement and I stand by it too. And they did not, but for the Bureau, and the Department of wishes to tristique blandit. As expected from the pellentesque. Sed gravida metus vitae felis fringilla molestie. Largest gate of the valley or the free layer. Live Laoreet innovative region carton antioxidants. Even football lion layer, but not long-sapien members. Listing weekend boat need. Bureau present propaganda porta receives the airline. Sometimes the sauce in the region, the need becomes a graduated Performance. Cras porttitor lorem at eros accumsan feugiat chocolate, iaculis rutrum from the television, in the greatest of the mass of hate, not the environment. Until it becomes a front for outdoor shooting.

AFTER FAME

[99]

'You wished for a hundred friends'
There were thousands planted
but at this rate I will starve
before a single leaf is released

The assembly of the major works from the period seemed less a linear route than an outward expansion, like the slow growth of a crystal. I heard soft thunder as I landed. In late October I'd headed west, to this wet, walled city, in order to better promote the archive's renovation. My luggage was yet to arrive, and for a few nights I occupied an empty house. My exact purpose remained mysterious; I suspected the posting was punishment for an indiscretion I was unsure I had committed.

[100]

Remember to give thanks
for the availability of conductive elements
Tungsten, tin, tantalum
and gold

Mornings I spent in the window of a coffee place, switching at lunchtime to the franchise opposite, to study where I'd sat: the angle of the chair, the stains and crumbs, roughly drafting my hour there. I stayed longer than necessary, hoping to arrive at a preference for one outlet or the other, preparing myself for the more taxing distinctions demanded by the archive. Often, on receiving the archive's directions, I would respectfully ask, 'Is this a test?' A vast amount of material in the region is yet to be catalogued.

[101]

The patron of my own reward
I felt I should faint
The book went to the infernal waters
Its other title is *Summer Day*

It was in this turbulent atmosphere that my adversary first identified himself. My decisive journey, described at the beginning of these notes, came at a time when I had become well known for the sophistication of my preferences, and had even, through vanity, sought to promote what some had called the fineness of my exclusions and additions by agreeing to a number of interviews and media features – an elevation of my persona I would come to regret. I visualise consciousness as a sort of pond-shaped, deepening dip.

[102]

I think you'll light
this image
with an expression
of indifference

My adversary emerged in the unlikely figure of a rival archivist. My adversary is a person who does not share my preferences; he had derived his pseudonym from an interest in contemporary communication and information theory. His first assault, a rewritten version of one of my own press releases, was calculated to reveal my unwitting or disguised support of certain hierarchical structures, which I had consistently claimed to undermine through my selections, and impacted significantly on a limited readership. But symbolically his act created a divide, which sided me firmly with an old, oppressive regime of preferences, while his mere statement of opposition, however unfounded or distorted, grouped him with the new, the unrepresented, the progressive.

[103]

To live once again in the right
you must abolish your laughter
reverse the story of our capture
Or millions can return the favour

I was plagued by dreams in which my notebooks had been annotated with detailed sketches of disembodied ears, so deeply inked their whorled reliefs felt realistic. Strangely, it was my rival's contacts among the archiving elites that were crucial to his sudden ascendency, information I gleaned from a mile-long email thread that would later prove invaluable. Revenge preoccupied me. For a fortnight I got high on cough syrup and bombed his coastal city in a flight sim.

[104]

Our mildness is not prepared for the necessary surgery
so we remain raptured
by our obscure designation
until we know how to serve

Isolated, without defenders, I brooded and considered a next move: a sort of sidestep by which I determined that my 'allegiance' to the governing criteria was loyalty in name only; with a scrupulousness I intended to become tiresome, and which did become tiresome, I cited pages of examples in which the subtlety of my revisions and omissions could only be said to have improved the range and intensity of the archive's make-up. This exhaustive and well-publicised response coincided with my adversary's first difficulties: in his new-found prominence he was now faced with the problem of having to be 'for' something, rather than simply against a casually denigrated authority, and it was at this moment his articulacy, so responsive until then, failed him.

[105]

The quotations take ages
losing their names and characteristics
so that the ancient materials
can remain without purpose

their pale shapes partially eroded
as figures turning away into darkness
whose actions won't be interpreted
and could be called anything

For a while I luxuriated in comfortable antagonism, marvelling at how each missile found its mark; from here the targets were so huge as to be unmissable. But it was only a matter of time before I was compelled to retake my position. My next set of approvals and rueful exclusions in the archive's project of diligent remapping was characterised by a deliberate, almost overstated hesitancy: gone were the bravado and assertiveness; here was a quieter, more reflective archivist, nominally selfless, allowing the interconnected field of preferences to play out in the zone of his attention.

[106]

Have you received water as a dainty offering,
perhaps as you are being driven by a friend
through the diluted evening towards a party
you have mixed feelings about, while wringing

from it all the promises you'd made previously,
and the night with its non-stop sighing has
the makings of a specific assault on your integrity . . .
I'm trying to hide my meaning

inside a kind of skewed personal allusion
but I actually have no idea what I'm talking about – sorry!
It's only a poem,
my dainty offering. See you in the morning.

My most successful manoeuvre was to situate some of these decisions conspicuously close to my adversary's outlying territory: by absorbing a few of his key assertions I was able to effectively disarm him, and in doing so I revealed a fissure in his impervious archivist-image. In the meantime, my possessions had arrived from the mainland, so my patient occupation of competing coffee franchises was over. Heralded by a procession across the dawn sky of legions of purple clouds, the white van appeared in an opportune, moonlit moment. Helping the driver unload, a twenty-stone insomniac wired on caffeine pills, who refused even a glass of water, I ruminated on the forgotten physical labour of moving and separating this half-ton of files and paper, a job that had already happened in the ether.

[107]

The suspicion
impossible to disregard
once it has arisen
that it is us who work for our servants

It didn't seem possible any longer to speak of a confrontation. The division was along the lines of the publicly visible: the reality was the representation. My work was not a matter of geography – all of which came as something of a relief. It now seemed possible to appreciate the utterances of power if they were genuinely arbitrary, and to ensure this in my own dealings, I devised a system of machine selection. My archive contributions became immediately esoteric, defying categorisation, and lost me a few friends I was grateful to be free of. Here, my thoughts return to my adversary, his darkness, his silence, as if in the elapse of a long heartbeat I've intuited his presence – and only now a hand is reaching, slowly, between us.

[108]

Hey. My poem says 'good morning' to
you – I hope to see you in the future –
are really beautiful. I approach your place
I look at the upper bay. I am an old man
in these districts that are emptied almost
I'm ready to migrate – move on, that is.
I get up early at home and so on
which is to say, it's worthwhile to get
distances – of what's too much, or
within reach. I don't own a toga, but if I did
I'd be wearing one. I pause often as the dawn
becomes available, as it has to – now
actually drawing near you, an hour is come.
My poem says 'good morning' from me.

[109]

What you should do if I complain like this is feel intense waves of sadness and joy. In those shorts, that ass is better than in Roman poems. Because none of my sighs are felt when you lie on your neck and capture an angle of yourself not falling sleep. I think that that ass might feel softer than nuzzling doves. I don't distract from your desire for a strained stomach if from above I drop praise, as I can see that that ass did not escape the notice of any exercise, that that ass is a credit to all girls and all women, so I let you know by liking it. If I put a paw to its haunch, you might threaten to depose: then it asks to be lifted. Chastity is great if you're a modest dog, I wouldn't know. That ass appears to be valuable like Indian pearl earrings that have never been found. Shoulders are thin like a girl's, while that ass is heavy: I think it asks to be lifted. If that's the story, you can put it on me whole. Maybe I'll just meet you. That ass is portrayed in a public setting, in various file types. Ass is possibly chained to a luxury tax scheme. Liking so much of what you see of that ass, it may be similar for anyone, either you or me, to look at it? Ass is fine; send the file, and thou shalt crop to view, each version is true to the real thing – I think both would make a great display picture.

[110]

I am writing to complain my poems are too long.
There is nothing I can possibly write in response.

[111]

My publishers are excellent judges of quality and character.
I hope you won't be too disappointed with their next offering:
'The new thing that's enough like the old thing to be accepted
yet also enough unlike it to satisfy the demand for novelty . . .'

[112]

My patron (who owns a Prius)
(just checking you're still awake)
re: a transaction on the dark web –
'The world is warm, opaque . . .'

[113]

Imagine you identified the traits you wanted to abandon . . .
I disown the poems published in the following journals
The Spectator, *nthposition*, *Lithub*, and one shortlisted
in the 2011 Adnams National Poetry Competition.

[114]

I lost all feeling in the water-meadows
after exiting the old neighbourhood without
even an explanatory message, opening
the door on a green blaze that echoed back
inside the house, an oval mirror bared
for an instant on the stairwell like a throat.
This isn't where I said I'd meet you, instead
I hoped you'd know me at my signal.
And it was not a good time to go out.
Birds hasten through trees in the valley
below, a breath of wind comes, as from the back
of a church. I'm a temporary and not at all
discontented inhabitant, a gardener, a guardian
of a vault, whose days happen to have fallen
in a particular pattern. And did you expect me
to renounce my connections? An absent patron
made me a custodian in his daughter's place,
the heiress and mystery author, already ashes.
Money still flies his way in the shadowy city . . .
With nothing to recommend me, how on earth
could I escape my reward? But that's not what
I talk about during my two-hour phone calls
on the solstice evenings, when I like to fall
asleep while watching many appalling films.

[115]

I kind of wants - envy, to go forward into tumult -
girl whiter than pale
silver, snow, lily, privet
a kind of darker than the night, but I want to,
the ant, or the pitch, rejecting, the grasshopper.
now you were contemplating, cruel, were you thinking about:
If I know you well, - some way off, to cause to tilt forward
or to advance to a great height -
you'll live, probably:.

[116]

I'm still here, Marcus, in the groves of Mars,
double-checking the triple-lock on the library,
observed by three reclining horses,
one quite pale. Beautiful acres of woodland
surround, and there's a scarily deep well.
If you look for long enough you can make out
a reflection in the trembling disc of black liquid,
staring back from the brink of the underworld.
This much alone, it's hard to feel entirely at ease.
I sometimes startle awake from nightmares.
His daughter's portraits are all taken away
but the novels line a low shelf in the study,
melodramatic titles that are not quite laughable . . .
Walking the grounds on morning errands
one often feels observed, an unsuspecting
character in one of the owner's elaborate plots . . .

[117]

I'm trying to interest my contacts in the gaming industry in a project I'm developing, working title: *Irretrievable*. It's still in pre-production, but the user journey unfolds something like this.

> After purchasing *Irretrievable* from a trusted application you are directed to a third-party website that hosts additional software you will need to download in order to patch *Irretrievable* for your operating system. After a couple of failed attempts (the software appears to download, but when the files are unzipped they are empty), you return to the application where you bought the game and access the troubleshooting guide, a 68-page PDF that you search for keyphrases such as 'patch software for [your OS] failed to execute', '[your OS] won't execute' and 'patch failed'. You return results in page range 12–25. Skim reading above and below the highlighted terms, you receive directions to a second third-party site which hosts the necessary software bundle in a newer build with fixes dated last month. Following the link you are redirected to a page with dense feeds of Russian text and a rash of pop-up animated RPG ads, which you shoot down in order of appearance. Retreating, you type the name of the second third-party site into the search bar manually and hit the first result. The page is tidy and legitimate looking, scrolling down you see lists of links to various patch solutions, the addresses commingling capitals and lowercase, followed by messes of numbers, horded in twin columns. You return to the initial installation instructions on the purchase page to locate the correct software package spec for your operating system, but when you come back to the second third-party website you quickly see that the particular build you require isn't listed. You click the search bar in the upper right of the third-party website's landing page and copy-paste the full name of the software

package you require. The results return a blog entry dated two weeks ago and you click it without reading the description properly, spotting the key words 'new' and 'fix'. The page looks promising – perhaps the admin simply forgot to update the list of links on the landing page. You slow down to make a more careful assessment: after a brief, friendly explanation there is a single hyperlink, the name of which matches the software patch you're searching for. The entry is tagged with the same nomenclature, as well as the year, the month, the word 'irretrievable', and the word 'fix'. You initiate the download, opting to observe its progress: the bar fills slowly, strugglingly for about ten seconds, the percentages stalling, before speeding significantly once it's about a quarter full. The whole operation takes less than a minute: swift, but not suspiciously so. The download unzips automatically and you see a trustworthy-looking desktop icon planted in the folder, which you open, following a conventional installation wizard, completed in six steps. You are advised to restart, which you do immediately. Once your computer is operational again you open the gaming application where you bought *Irretrievable* and go straight to your purchases folder. You double click on the *Irretrievable* application icon: pumice and smart purple, it's an indistinct composition which doesn't resolve into a meaningful representation in the few seconds you spend examining it while waiting for the game to boot up. The desktop icon of the additional software you just successfully installed balloons in your sidebar and floats up and down, then freezes before vanishing. A brick of plain text appears unceremoniously, black on a light grey background.

> Congratulations, you've unlocked phase two. *Irretrievable* is one of the few anti-smart, user-reliant games on the market, and from now on your progress will demand a more concerted investment. (1) locate a document of some tangible value, practical, personal or otherwise, on your hard-drive. Here are

pathways to three suggestions our algorithms have generated during a quick scan. (2) Rename the document <retrieved_erotion_b1p117118l58> and move it to your desktop. (3) Follow <u>this</u> hyperlink, and agree to collect the document it requests. (4) Save it to your desktop. (5) When asked you if you wish to keep both the document you're downloading and the one you already have in that location that shares its name, select *replace*.

> Your task is to retrieve the information you've just erased, using any means at your disposal. It will take two-to-four hours of sustained concentration, if it's even possible. If and when it is returned, the information that once belonged to you will have been radically transformed. We don't know how, or what it will cost you.

>To opt out: in *SAFE MODE* (ISBN 0993569331) turn to line 4, page 22. Write the keyphrase in the space below, detach this page and return it to the publisher by post with your bank details for a full refund.

[118]

Haven't you had enough poems yet?
Because 118 of these is probably my limit.
Perhaps I can recommend some further reading.

Further reading

13:50
so we want to lesson things
13:52
so the process of this being just copy those are really for me useful blog
14:00
where God is attempted to translate in about two thousand five a lot of the
14:05
programs and marshal and so I copy and paste the Latin explore it is a google
14:12
time slide here is an attempt to translate latin but it doesn't have the
14:16
is getting better i think but it doesn't really have the capabilities
14:19
probably so be there like scaffolds that I would then be sort of built our
14:24
something just came up with something like the interesting automatically and
14:31
certainly not going to read out a number so like 12 the computer and not just
14:37
chillin pause and us are skating by fast mr. question I want to be with you
14:44
wherever you go back to partying for getting medical regular shows and stop
14:49
checking your fighting for a second
14:50
you need a new distraction nada guys want any by real book and one of the
14:56
city
14:56
I'm pocket-sized you want to show life
15:01
a solitary going normal white girls I clean or smoked by the mailbox crowd or
15:06
you sorted out of readings much but if someone calls you a genius you get to
15:10
kiss them and I said the wrong things like an hour 5 stars
15:14
now that you've divided on the fair market international now that you have

15:19
reproduced second printing but also often even suffer races contracture
15:24
artistic or otherwise
15:26
I suppose you've earned that side shot to scare away slaughter like an invoice
15:30
I'll go back to your right
15:34
drop the little mind routes and reciting your face when you choose to pick up my
15:38
book The Book of trials joke book
15:41
I think this is your expression change on the cover of the book of lamentations
15:47
there's no shame in nomination or expression be in my book the book
15:53
censorship is quite amusing reading the book division in lactating isn't i'm
15:59
going to be really mindful of the bones while lying supine on the crimson cypher
16:03
with the latest recipe of your aisle is where an expression like the color
16:08
it's blank my life proves it my father is a harmless around eight highs in the
16:16
wheel arch on the flight to Hawaii
16:18
otherwise alive Apone stops the time coming up for a picture to be taken
16:23
I myself become more faithful heights the question is then what happens
16:28
arg cancer is very smaller little say older
16:32
there's got to be safe
16:35
that should be followed to the letter just try to be sensible I guess remain
16:40
vigilant between street bodies may spread down a dark corridors orgy much
16:45
attention to yourself

16:47
he finds the starting fights and running away or better yet deny everything he's
16:52
done I believe that police had to protect us
16:55
I do not feel your hands my prayers or presence
17:00
I know it isn't fair instead of a kiss nothing is likely than getting your path
17:06
however far and a while is always more flash the car is stuck to my partner if
17:13
I was of money comes out
17:15
the wall why I of all the bill even when it isn't on paid absolutely abstract
17:21
I get to my friends as well and in the event of the unthinkable
17:25
I'm prepared the face and that's the muscle the freedom to write bad Collins
17:34
media
17:34
opponents only one state that's what about is you guys on your grandfather's
17:40
freedom
17:42
1x myself the lifestyle not gettin myself
17:48
you vs for the low stalled on corrupt the high style a pair days we just need
17:55
to be corrupted
17:56
the lifestyle is Denise the relation it corrects like money incorrectly itself
18:04
fame is such a sweet draft digitally it crashes the blood we can swing it
18:10
countries with the poet's claim when the surveillance state connected into
18:18
looking cells and the screens finally resolve us the first ones to banish
18:22
always journalists
18:25
meanwhile the press and Harvey development books a total isolation

18:29
arms or secret services I suppose each will go after their own each of the
18:37
people with books
18:39
this is at the heart of the service of learning there's no need to be shy in
18:43
front of the elderly is all these literary parties every kind of Spain
18:48
surely waits outside with a little glass vial to carry off the prize of your BTW
18:54
that by saving you the trouble
18:56
content to London needed so on by yourself
19:00
now start living in paper as a flame does ashes of election
19:10
I promise when you cut your hair and curls fall too many more with the filthy
19:14
leaves the stairs of boys and bells will arrive like knives and a white neck
19:20
he revealed the mystery two vessels and with each looks on guest star lines
19:26
again
19:27
they're coming angular is again in the girls full the last week's as a teenager
19:33
that's a lot of this time slowly like early twenties
19:39
all right versus from y equals not for a teacher's dictating class
19:45
these arms why is coming without a penis please
19:49
well with your other having write down words that's a nice song new dresses and
19:53
petticoats these days anyway
19:55
this will always get into the arms of members who had us some more programs
20:00
you can spare yourself the severity of all of the castration complex is in the

20:05
works and look for yourself also expect my stuff back to me sign in under one
20:16
hour
20:18
ok

Index of first lines